LIVING WITH ALCOHOLISM

DEALING WITH THE DAMAGING EFFECTS IN YOUR LIFE AND THE LIVES OF THOSE YOU LOVE

Copyright 2009
KMS Publishing.com

You never imagined your life would turn out this way? Is your life controlled by alcohol? Are you an alcoholic? Do you live with an alcoholic? Do you know someone who is?

Alcoholism is a chronic disease, with its own symptoms, its own devastating effects on lives and its treatment & prevention methods.

Learn to take control again…get your life back; get your love one back! This book is your complete guide to cope with alcoholism in your life.

Educate yourself on alcoholism as a chronic disease, study the symptoms checklist and alcoholic profile so you can detect the early warning signs. Learn how to handle an alcoholic spouse, how to take care of yourself within the situation, what you can do to help and what you cannot do. Be aware of coping techniques and life management strategies that can aid you in managing daily life with alcoholism. Discover support groups that can help you and the victim in your life overcome alcoholism.

Plus numerous more information inside the pages of this book. Eradicate the harmful effects of alcoholism in your life and the life of those you love!

TABLE OF CONTENTS

INTRODUCTION

Living with an alcoholic in your life can make life seem impossible. Every day you are walking on eggshells. Life may be stressful, uncertain, or just plain bad. One thing is certain. It is never easy living with an alcoholic in your life.

Living with an alcoholic means that you have a person in your life who you cannot count on. If this person is a spouse then you have someone who should have you as a priority but has alcohol as a priority instead. You cannot count on this person even for day to day tasks because you never know when the need for alcohol will interfere with their life and with yours and you will have to pick up the slack.

Alcohol creates distance. When a person is so totally focused on obtaining and imbibing alcohol then that becomes the main relationship in that person's life. It is not their significant other, their children, or even their job. The one relationship is the one that they have with alcohol. All their desire, all their effort goes into their dance with alcohol. Everything else becomes secondary.

This dependence upon alcohol turns your every interaction with this person into a struggle. This constant push and pull is one that you cannot win.

The siren call of drinking is too loud to be drowned out by voices not firmly lodged in the alcoholic's head. You may scream for hours, but the voices inside the alcoholic's head which tell them to drink never stop. You can try, but you will tire long before the desire for alcohol does.

Life can be challenging without having someone with a substance abuse problem in your life. With an alcoholic, life can be unbearable. You never know which face the person will show or how the person will react in any circumstance. You never know if you can depend upon this person or if you will have to pick up the slack.

The question becomes one of practicality. How do you survive living with an alcoholic in your life? Do you go to great lengths to convince this person to change? Do you leave this person to hit rock bottom and to realize the insidiousness of their dependence upon alcohol? Do you run around trying to shield them from the effects of their drinking so that they do not hurt themselves too badly?

These are difficult questions with complex answers. Only you can look at your situation and your needs to answer them. Some courses of action will help to bring about the changes you want while others will only help everyone involved to become more firmly entrenched in their roles. To understand what living with an alcoholic in your life means and what to do about it, you need to take a closer look at the issues that surround and underlie these behaviours.

I.

THE DISEASE OF ALCOHOLISM

Alcoholism is a disease. It is a chronic disease that creates a physiological state where a person's body is actually dependent upon alcohol. Without this alcohol this person's body will have difficulty functioning and will experience any number of withdrawal symptoms. The problem, however, extends far beyond the physical. Trying to get into the alcoholic's head and to see through his or her eyes is a good first step.

The Addiction

When you are an alcoholic, your desire for alcohol may very well come to overtake your life. You may find yourself constantly thinking about your last drink, your current drink, and where your next drink will come from. You may come to plan your life around the availability of alcohol. You may progress to a point where you hide or lie about your drinking just so that you can continue these addictive patterns without anyone knowing. In short, you may become obsessed.

Whether you realize it or not, you may lose control. You may find it impossible to go any length of time without having a drink. You might begin to start making deals with yourself and your loved ones to go without drinking for a period of time only to find that you go back on your word.

The Denial Syndrome

You may rationalize it away by thinking that you do not have a problem, that you should be allowed to have a drink and that your problems make the alcohol necessary. You will tell yourself anything as long as it leads to you getting another drink.

Your life may begin to deteriorate. You may begin missing work or performing below the standards that you once lived up to. You may begin to distance yourself from friends and loved ones so that they will not realize the extent of your drinking.

Worst of all, you may develop a severe drinking problem but still be able to maintain your life. Sometimes your problem with alcohol can co-exist with your normal life. You may be an alcoholic who makes it to work every day, spends time with your family, and fulfils all your obligations. You can do all this and still be living with a chronic disease that no one knows about but you.

Mental Blankness

Alcoholism is a disease that is about more than just drinking. It is about more than missing out on plans and special events in the lives of your loved ones. It is about missing out on life for as long as you continue to drink. You are not there for those you love, and you are not there for yourself. You are trapped in a world of pain. You may try to get out time and time again, but your every effort may fail. In short, you feel like there is be nothing you can do.

Your loved one with alcoholism becomes trapped in the push and pull between wanting a normal, healthy life and feeling the physiological need for alcohol. Fighting this addiction can seem to be an insurmountable obstacle. It might seem easier to give in, and this is what many do.

Beyond fearing for the alcoholic's relationships is the fear for his or her health and life. Alcohol damages the body as much as it wounds the soul. Knowing the possible physical consequences of prolonged heavy drinking can further drive home the seriousness of alcoholism.

Health Dangers

Consuming excessive amounts of alcohol over time can lead to any number of health problems. Not everyone who consumes large amounts of alcohol will experience the same health problems, but no one who continues heavy consumption of alcohol over time escapes unaffected.

Overconsumption of alcohol can lead to alcoholic hepatitis. This is a type of inflammation of your liver. Its symptoms can include nausea, vomiting, abdominal tenderness, and loss of appetite. This may then progress to cirrhosis. Cirrhosis is a condition wherein liver tissue can sustain extensive damage. This damage is irreversible.

A healthy liver usually transforms nutrients into forms that your body can use, produces bile to aid in digestion of fat, and regulates the amount of sugar in your bloodstream. These and other tasks carried out by the liver cannot be carried out as well or possibly at all when your liver tissue has sustained enough damage due to alcohol abuse.

Alcoholism can also create gastrointestinal problems. This may include an inflammation in your stomach lining or actual tears in the upper portion of your stomach as well as the lower portion of your esophageal tissue. You may have difficult absorbing b vitamins into your bloodstream.

Excessive drinking may also be destructive to your pancreas. Ordinarily, your pancreas serves the functions of making insulin and glucagon to keep your metabolism within a normal range, and produces enzymes that help you to digest protein, fat and, carbohydrates. As your pancreas is damaged, your body loses the ability to complete these tasks. You cannot digest protein, fat, and carbohydrates as efficiently and consequently have more trouble receiving the nutrition you need to maintain normative bodily functions.

Excessive drinking can also contribute to high blood pressure and damage your heart. These circumstances can increase your risk for heart failure or stroke.

Alcohol is especially problematic if you have diabetes. Alcohol interferes with the release of insulin form your liver and may increase your chances of experiencing hypoglycemia. If you are already taking medications to lower your blood sugar level then this side effect may cause serious health complications.

As you continue to consume large amounts of alcohol over an extended period of time you may come to experience neurological problems. You may damage your nervous system to the length that your hands and feet become numb. The damage could go so far as to cause you to experience disordered thinking and even dementia as a result of your drinking.

Finally, you may have an increased chance of contracting certain types of cancers. Cancer of the esophagus, larynx, colon, and liver have been linked to overconsumption of alcohol.

Of course, you may not actually be the one with the drinking problem. You may be on the outside looking in. Being in this position can leave you feeling helpless. Knowing that these health problems are the natural results of excessive consumption of alcohol can leave you feeling powerless as you know that the alcoholic in your life is marching steadily toward a future rife with medical problems.

These medical problems can disrupt your life even if the alcoholic becomes sober. They are the consequences of all the years spent drinking. Even after the alcoholism has been dealt with, assuming you are lucky enough to see the alcoholic in your life maintain sobriety, then these after effects will still have to be handled. Even if the drinking is halted, the damage may already have been done.

Relationship Problems

The effects of alcohol are far-reaching. The health consequences may be more quantifiable, but the social effects are just as devastating. Alcoholism leaves in its trail broken promises, shattered relationships, and a life empty of everything but alcohol. In time, it leaves an alcoholic with nothing.

Alcoholism does not happen in a bubble. It is not only the alcoholic who must deal with the ramifications of this single-minded focus. Family, friends, and co-workers are all affected. There is no such thing as an alcoholic who keeps all the effects of alcoholism to himself or herself.

II.

THE PROFILE OF AN ALCOHOLIC

So how can you tell if a loved one or co-worker is an alcoholic? Where is the line between someone who enjoys a few drinks after work or who just likes to have a good time and someone who has a serious substance abuse problem? It can be hard to tell.

Either one is likely to reassure you that their behaviour is normal and acceptable. Either one could say that they just had a long day, week, or year and just needed a night out. Either one could say that they went too far just this once and will never do it again. Part of your question becomes, will they do it again?

First, you want to consider the ramifications of posing this possibility to someone. If you do suspect that someone is an alcoholic, do you confront them? Will this encourage a genuine alcoholic to get help, or will it merely inform them that they need to put more effort into covering their tracks?

Many people do not wish to intervene if they suspect that someone they know is an alcoholic. It is easier to tell yourself that your friend, co-worker, or lover is not really an alcoholic. They do not really have a problem. They just felt bad last night, or maybe they were celebrating.

Maybe they have always been a drinker and the slide into alcoholism was slow and subtle. Maybe you do not want to admit it. Why would anyone not want to admit that there is a problem? Maybe this denial feels more comfortable because if someone you know has a problem with drinking then you have a problem too.

You know that you cannot have a healthy relationship with an alcoholic. It does not matter if this person is a spouse, family member, friend, or co-worker. You cannot escape the fact that alcoholism will affect your relationship. If your relationship with this person is limited then you may be able to ignore the shifts in personality and the inconsistencies in behaviour. If the person is closer to you then you cannot avoid the alcoholism. You can shut your eyes and pretend that nothing has changed or that this is temporary but you know better. This is a disease that spreads though everything the alcoholic touches.

Functioning Alcoholics

Again, part of the problem is that not every alcoholic has a life that is falling apart. Many do, but many do not. The term is functioning alcoholic. Many alcoholics can get through the days without any problems. They can do their work, spend time with family and friends, and still maintain excessive drinking patterns. So how do you know if someone is an alcoholic when they have a life that, other than their excessive consumption of alcohol, looks fine?

Identifying an alcoholic is about more than just going down a checklist. This can be a helpful tool, but first you have to be willing to face the possibly ugly truth. Someone you know may be an alcoholic. They may have a disease that could very well kill them. They may have a disease and they might not want your help.

Suspicion Is A Great Initial Warning Tool

You have to start somewhere. A good place to start is your suspicion that someone may be an alcoholic. You know this person and you know what typical behavior for this person. If you have been around to witness the descent or to witness the differences in this person then you can tell when that person is no longer acting like they used to act.

You can tell when this person started putting the consumption of alcohol above his or her own best interests. You want to begin here, with your own intimate knowledge of the individual's life. The next thing you want to look for is the presence of the common symptoms. These hallmarks of alcoholism will help you to support your sense that something could be very wrong.

The Alcoholic Symptoms Checklist

You want to remember that not everyone will have all of the symptoms or even the same symptoms. People can manifest alcoholism in different ways. You do not want to dismiss the possibility that someone you know may have a problem with alcohol even though they do not adhere to a checklist of symptoms. There are also different degrees of substance abuse problems. Alcoholism is just the fully realized manifestation of problems with alcohol consumption.

Many who are alcoholics will deny that there is a problem. They will generate all sorts of excuses and explanations for their drinking. This makes it harder to identify when there is a problem. You may not want to admit that there is a problem and this can make their explanations seem all the more plausible.

Withdrawal Symptoms

For starters, alcohol is a drug. When someone who is dependent upon a drug does not have access to a drug then they get withdrawal symptoms. Someone who is dependent upon alcohol who is then denied access to alcohol for any length of time may manifest some or all of the following symptoms.

They may become nervous, irritable, depressed, tired, or have trouble thinking clearly. Physically, they may get a headache, exhibit hand tremors, or have trouble sleeping. Also, a person in alcohol withdrawal might experience sweating, nausea, loss of appetite, vomiting, rapid heart rate, or a pale complexion. In extreme cases, an individual in withdrawal may have a fever, convulsions, hallucinations, or blackouts where they experience gaps in their memory.

Increased Tolerance Level To Alcohol

The development of an increased tolerance to alcohol is another symptom of alcoholism. The body adjusts to the amounts of alcohol that it receives so it requires greater amounts to feel the same effect. If a person is developing a tolerance to alcohol then this may be a sign that this person is becoming or has become an alcoholic.

Pre-Emptive Drinking Patterns To Cope With Life

Another symptom of alcoholism is when a person starts to drink when they are by themselves. The act of drinking without a social event or without being in a social setting can be an indicator of alcoholism. The same is true for those who drink before a social event just to make sure that they are relaxed for that event. This pre-emptive drinking demonstrates that the person is using alcohol to cope with life.

When someone starts to use alcohol as a tool to deal with life, the negative parts or the positive ones, then this is a good indicator that their drinking is becoming a problem. This is true when a person drinks to deal with or to forget about any problems they have because they had a bad day or week. Drinking alcohol is not a healthy way to deal with emotional stress.

Secretive Behavior Like Sneaking And Hiding Alcohol

As an alcoholic's drinking problem progresses then they will probably begin to hide their drinking. It is likely that at some point someone has noticed their excessive drinking and pointed it out. This may have happened multiple times which makes it even more likely that the alcoholic has taken steps to hide their drinking. Secretive behaviors such as hiding alcohol and sneaking off to drink without being open and honest about it are definite calling cards of a drinking problem.

Intentions To Get Drunk

When a person states that their intention when drinking is to get drunk then this is another big indicator that there is a problem. Consuming alcohol quickly especially with the intention of inebriation is a warning sign. This person may begin drinking before everyone else, may drink more alcohol faster than everyone else, and may continue drinking after everyone else has stopped. When this happens, there is a problem. Drinking to get drunk should tip you off that something is not right.

Defensive Reactions When Confronted

An alcoholic is likely to deny that there is a problem if confronted. They may become agitated or react violently to questions about their drinking. This defensive reaction is not a good sign. If someone does not have a problem drinking then it is unlikely that they will overreact to questioning about it. On the other hand, some alcoholics will calmly dismiss such claims in an attempt to avoid the issue. Remember, every alcoholic is different.

Your suspicion regarding your loved one or co-worker will provide a large part of your proof that something is wrong. If you are worried that something is wrong then that is often a good indication that something is wrong. If you catch them in a lie about drinking or if you have to lie about their drinking then that is another clear indicator. People tend to lie when they have something to hide.

Alcoholism Interferes With Life

Similarly, if you ever have to change your plans because of a person's drinking, that is yet another sign. When drinking gets to the point where it interferes with life, you need to do something about it.

There are many questions that will lead you to see the truth of the situation. Do you ever feel that you have to modify your behavior or be careful because you are afraid that the other person will drink if you upset them? Have you been embarrassed by the potential alcoholic in your life because of their drinking? Have you been hurt because of their drinking? Have you found or looked for hidden alcohol? Has the person ever driven after drinking? Are you adversely affected in any way by this person's drinking? If you are honest with yourself about the answers, these questions will tell you all you need to know.

III.
COPING WITH ALCOHOLISM IN A MARRIAGE

Living with an alcoholic in your life is difficult, but what if that alcoholic is more than an acquaintance? What if the alcoholic is your spouse? Trying to broach the topic of alcoholism is hard enough with someone you barely know. How do you handle alcoholism when it is in your own home and sleeps in your bed with you every night?

Being married to an alcoholic is a tricky situation. You need to get to a point where you realize the truth and figure out how to face it. Denial, although easier at first, will not solve the problem. Problems as big as this one do not go away on their own.

There is another concern. If you are living with an alcoholic then it is probably not just their problem. Odds are, you have been brought into the mix somehow and are playing a role in this drama. Alcoholism does not develop overnight. It usually begins with more innocent drinking that grows into an addiction over time.

Your Role As Spouse To An Alcoholic

Because you share a life with this person, you play a part in this drama of alcoholism. You are not to blame. You must always remember that even though you play a part. You are not to blame for someone else's drinking problem. You only look at the role you play so that you can choose a healthier one both for yourself and your spouse.

When you are married to an alcoholic, it is likely that you have been called in to protect your alcoholic spouse, probably more than once. You may have had to cover up for bad behaviour, for missed social events, or just as an accomplice who sits by as though nothing is wrong as each drink is consumed. You feel like something is wrong, you know that something is wrong, and you watch the problems unfold.

It may be worse. You may be drinking with your alcoholic spouse in addition to other behaviors. This can make it hard to talk to your spouse about their drinking when you were the one drinking along with them.

Helping Your Spouse

Still, whether you drink or not, alcoholism must be identified and faced. You cannot let guilt keep you from trying to help someone you love.

You may be taking a more direct approach. You could be making outright demands that your alcoholic spouse change their drinking patterns. If your insistence that your spouse quit drinking solves the problem then that is a miracle.

Alcoholics need professional help. There may be anecdotes of those who quit alone, but they are the minority. Alcoholism is a disease. It is bigger than just you, your spouse, or your marriage. It is not a question of your partner being able to love you enough to quit but a question of what it really takes to become sober.

The shame of alcoholism can lead to increased isolation. As friends and extended family realize that the problem exists then they may shy away from social activities, or the alcoholic may tire of ongoing questioning regarding his or her behaviour. The alcoholism is ingrained and seen as necessary to the one suffering from it so anyone who suggests another way of living is a threat to it.

You may become depressed. Repeated attempts to help your spouse, if they are unsuccessful, can wear you down. You want to help, but you may not know how to do it. Many alcoholics refuse help even as their lives fall to pieces. Many have the best of intentions yet continue to perpetuate the patterns that have been dominating their lives for so long.

The alcoholism becomes all consuming. Your partner cannot see beyond his or her addiction, and you feel like the unwanted third wheel in your own marriage. It has become about more than alcoholism. Your marriage could be in trouble because your spouse is in trouble and is taking you down too.

Knowing What You Can And Cannot Do To Help Is Crucial

Knowing what to do in a situation that is this rife with emotion can be a challenge. You know what you want to do. You want to help your partner to end the alcoholism, but is it that simple? What can you do to help, and what things are impossible for you to do to help? Knowing the line between being supportive and giving too much is crucial.

Realize That You Cannot Fix The Problem On Your Own

You cannot control another human being. Do not even try. This is especially true in the case of an alcoholic. This does not mean that you should not make efforts to help, but realize that you cannot control an alcoholic. If you try to then you will make yourself angry, depressed, and burn yourself out.

This is not to say that you should stand by and do nothing while your spouse is a victim of alcoholism. It just means that you should not expect to be able to control the situation. You are not in control. When you accept this, you will stop making yourself feel worse for not being able to fix it on your own.

Do Not Protect The Alcoholic From The Outcome Of Their Actions

Do not shield the alcoholic from the repercussions of his or her actions. You may want to help the alcoholic to maintain their life and to keep up appearances, but this may actually prove counterproductive. Some alcoholics begin to see the effects of their actions when lives begin to fall apart around them.

If you run around holding everything together then this realization may never come. You have no doubt heard of people who are able to turn their lives around only once they hit rock bottom. This may be true.

If you continually shield a person from the consequences of his or her actions then you may also shield them from the reasons to change those actions. You may keep your spouse from seeing the truth and from wanting a new life badly enough to do something about it.

Keep In Mind That You Are Not A Victim Too

Do not make yourself into a victim. You are in control of your life. You may not be in control of another person's life, but you are always in control of yours. Make yourself aware that you are constantly making choices. They may not be pleasant ones and they may not seem like much, but they are your choices to make. You are not a victim in this.

Falling into this role just allows the problem to continue and possibly get worse. If you assume this position then you are only helping to perpetuate the downfall of both your lives. Even if you cannot make much of a difference to help the alcoholic in your life, you can still make changes to your own life.

Make sure that you are taking care of yourself and the others in your life. Focusing your entire life around someone else's problem will wear you down and when you are worn down and unhappy then you are unable to give yourself fully to anyone. Your job will probably suffer as will your relationships. You can offer help to the alcoholic, but you need to take care of yourself. That is one thing that you can do.

To this end, you want to refuse to put up with any negative effects of the alcoholics actions. When you allow the alcoholic to harm you, either directly and deliberately or indirectly and by accident, then you communicate to that person that his or her actions are okay. You make it acceptable to treat you in this manner. You make it acceptable to continue the drinking. You make it acceptable for this person to take your dignity as they lose their own.

Make The Conscious Effort To Deal With Abuse

These abusive actions must not be tolerated. It is your responsibility to confront the alcoholic with the consequences of their actions. If the abuse is a more direct kind, such as physical abuse, then it is your responsibility to remove yourself from the situation immediately. If there are children involved then you have a responsibility to remove them from the situation too. If you stay then you are choosing to be abused. You know that if it happens once then it will more than likely happen again.

Abuse is not a one time occurrence. It is a cycle. It repeats. If you allow it to happen once then it may very well happen again. And again.

It is easy to find yourself consumed by your spouse's alcoholism. It is such a large and looming problem that it can overtake your thoughts, your days, and your life. You may find yourself becoming isolated because you are devoting so much time to your relationship with the alcoholic.

You may be running around trying to make everything okay, or you may be having constant fights over the repercussions of their alcoholism. Either way, you are being consumed by the addiction just as surely as your spouse is being overtaken. You need to know more in life than the after-effects of alcoholism.

Make The Effort To Socialize And Connect With People Outside The Situation

Make new friends or reconnect with old ones. This may sound simplistic, but it is vital. With an alcoholic spouse, your world can get smaller and smaller. Your view of the world can become distorted as all that you know is the darker sides of life.

By connecting with those who exist outside of this situation, you can not only have a break from the distorted and stressful lifestyle of an alcoholic, you can remember what life was meant to be. You will have parts of your life where you are not caught up in the constant drama that is alcoholism. You will not be spending all your time around someone who is searching for their next drink or trying to explain why they had the last one.

You can try out new fun things with these friends or on your own. Your spouse's world may be growing tinier by the day, but yours does not have to do the same. Rediscover the joy in life. Seek out new experiences. Your life must march on, and you would do well to create fulfilling parts of your life even if at this point in time your alcoholic spouse cannot join you in these endeavours.

Make The Effort To Move Forward With Your Own Life

When your spouse is an alcoholic then there are probably many who collaborate to keep this dysfunction going. As you take the time to improve your own life, you may come to discover that there are other destructive relationships in your life that could be holding you back from a full life. Taking a second look at these relationships is an essential part of you moving forward.

Make changes to make your own life healthy from your relationships to your eating and exercise. If you choose to allow your life to become limited to the point where it is overrun by your alcoholic spouse then that is your choice, and it is a choice. You will not only be contributing to your spouse's alcoholic patterns, but you will be destroying your own life and health in the process.

No one is asking you to pretend that there is no problem or that you will not be affected by it. You just need to realize that the problem of alcoholism is theirs. Your partnership does mean that you are in it together to an extent, but you have your own life.

Your life is your responsibility just as their life is their responsibility. Both of you have a responsibility to take care of your own lives. If you do not then you will not have a chance of helping the other if and when they can admit that they need help.

The end point is this. You cannot control your spouse's life. You can be supportive without protecting them from repercussions, and you can be there without being consumed. The one thing that you do have control over is your life. Make your life into one that brings you happiness.

IV.
THE DAMAGING EFFECTS OF ALCOHOL ON CHILDREN

The effects of alcoholism on children are too many to mention. How can the mind of a child wrap itself around alcoholism? How can a child deal with the fact that they have a parent who is either present and out of control or just absent? How can a child have a sense of self-worth when a parent's first concern is not their welfare but is getting his or her next drink?

The effects of alcoholism on children are insidious. Children are not independent. Children cannot just walk out when things get too bad. They are entirely dependent on their parents, and those parents may not even be able to take care of themselves. Even worse, alcoholic parents may take the pain of their situation and turn it toward the ones who cannot defend themselves.

Children are totally dependent on their parents. They are at the mercy of parents whether those parents are loving and kind or uncaring substance abusers. Children are taught to obey their parents, to respect them. They are taught that parents know best. If they have a parent who does not care about them or who is abusive towards them then they may accept that that is what it best. They will feel that they deserve it.

Children do not understand why things happen. When bad things happen, children must either accept that the world is out of control or they must blame themselves. Accepting that they have no control over what happens to them is often more than a child's mind can bear. The child in a case such as this will often blame themselves. They will feel that they were not quiet enough, that they were not loved enough, that they are not good enough.

At least when they blame themselves they have control. They can believe that if only they were better then they would not have a parent who is drunk all the time or who is angry all the time. If only they try hard enough then they could stop the world from being so uncertain and unkind. Sadly, it was never their fault, and there is nothing they can do.

It gets worse. The child and parent relationship is the first way that someone learns about love. If a child experiences attention only through abuse then abuse may become inextricably attached to love in that child's mind. If a parent is absent then the child may feel alone and undeserving of love.

The child of an alcoholic never knows safety. Even if a situation is not physically abusive then there is emotional abuse. The parent will almost unfailingly veer toward either abuse or neglect. The alcohol in this situation has long since been more important than the child. The child is too easy to either be the target for all the blame for the problems in life or to be put on the back burner indefinitely because the pursuit of alcohol is not furthered by caring for the child.

A childhood with an alcoholic parent feels interminable, and in many ways it is. A child does not grow up, forget, and move on. Even without the conscious memories, this individual continues to live in the shadow of a childhood wherein they never new safety, security, consistency, or real love.

If a person does not know what any of these things look like then it can be hard to build an adult life that has them. They may recreate a life with the same uncertainty and abuse of their childhoods. Even worse, they may take their pain and pass it on.

Possible Problems Of Children Of Alcoholics

Children of alcoholics may have any of a multitude of possible problems. Children have to deal with situations that would be trying for adults, only they do not have the resources to frame the problems. They cannot stand back and take a logical look at what is going on. There are no rational explanations in the mind of a child.

Children are dependent upon those who harm them when their parents are abusive. The harm may come in different forms, but no alcoholic parent can properly care for children. No alcoholic parent can be present and supportive of their children as long as they are the victim of this heinous disease. It is not possible. You cannot provide a healthy environment for children if you do not begin with a health environment.

The underlying feelings of problems experienced by children of alcoholics follow familiar patterns. The manifestations vary, but the underlying issues are the same.

Guilt And Self-Blame

The child feels guilty. Whether directly blamed for the negative effects of the parent's alcoholism or not, the child attributes these effects to himself or herself. Children cannot step back and see that the alcoholism has nothing to do with them.

They can only look at others in the world who are not treated in the same way and come to the conclusion that they must be doing something to bring it about. If only they were better then they would not be treated in this way. They feel it is their fault.

Crippled Sense Of Self-Worth

A child believes that if they were only better, if they were only good enough, then their parent would not have to drink so much. This cripples a child's sense of self-worth. They measure their worth by something they cannot control. If they cannot change their situation, which they cannot, then they will never be able to believe that their life has worth.

Constant Fear And Worry

The child feels fear. With an uncertain home life, the child may worry constantly. This child will never know what to expect from a parent as he or she arrives at home. They do not know if the parent will be happy or angry or distant. They do not know if they should expect violence at home or if the alcoholic parent has become sick or injured a as result of the drinking. They do not know if the parent will be there.

The child will worry about their parent's marriage if this alcoholism has lead to fights. The child will also be afraid to ask for help. As terrible as it is to have an alcoholic parent, for a child having no parent at all feels like the end of the world. Even if that parent is an alcoholic.

No Stable Home Structure

Children thrive in an environment with structure. An alcoholic cannot provide that structure. When alcohol is the priority then children cannot be. A parent cannot simultaneously be an alcoholic and provide a stable, loving home environment. It just cannot be done.

Mistrust

An inability to trust others can stem from these inconsistencies. A child may isolate from others because of many reasons when living in an alcoholic household. The reasons begin with the shame of holding this terrible secret and wanting to keep it.

Close friends will want to come over to their friend's house but doing so would reveal the truth of the situation. This mistrust is carried into other relationships. If the child's first relationships, the ones with his or her parents, could not be trusted then how can the child be expected to be able to trust anyone?

Anger/ Depression

Anger and depression are common feelings too. The child will be angry at the parent for not being a more ideal, loving parent. Because of the powerlessness and hopelessness of the situation, the child will become depressed. He or she is caught in a bad place and has no way to get out of it. He or she learns that she is helpless, and this feeling of helplessness extends far beyond the home. This child feels that he or she can never hope to improve their life. If it could not be done at home then how could it be done anywhere else?

Rebellious Behavior

There are also more tangible manifestations of a child having one or more alcoholic parents. A child who starts failing at school is common with these circumstances. This could include the child skipping school. Other unlawful behaviour may accompany the truancy. The child may engage in behaviors ranging from stealing to acts of violence. It may not escalate to violence but may instead be shown as feelings and actions indicating aggression toward others.

Isolation And Social Withdrawal

Withdrawal from friends and social situations may result from having alcoholic parents. The combination of an inability to trust others coupled with the shame of a destructive home situation often leads to a distancing from other people. Feeling unworthy, unwanted, and unloved does not go away. If your parents could not love you then who could?

Suicidal Tendencies And Attempts

Finally, of course all this stress and negative emotion can lead to depression and thoughts of suicide. In some cases, suicide may be attempted. Feelings of worthlessness and helplessness often accompany thoughts of and attempts of suicide.

Obsessive Control To Change Their Life

Not all children of alcoholic families cope by acting out. Some go in the other direction. They may become the parental figures that they lack. They may become mature, responsible overachievers. They will work hard to receive impressive marks in school and use their control over themselves to attempt to solidify family living.

This control coexists with the distance found in a more obviously troubled youth. In this way, the damage that has been done to them may go underground for some time. The problems may only begin to surface after they have reached adulthood.

Adult Children Of Alcoholics

The problems that children face as a result of being children of alcoholics do not end with childhood. Issues that are not faced and dealt with do not simply disappear. They manifest in various ways and will continue to do so, interfering with the adult's life until the issues are uncovered and resolved.

The unspoken rules that are instituted for these children are carried into adulthood. They learn early on that no one can be trusted and that saying what they feel or think makes the world unsafe. While the life that this adult now leads may not have the same dangers as the childhood did, these rules live on.

It is a case of an adult living with rules that were created by a child's mind and that are sustained by a child's fear. Any violation of these rules can instantly return the adult to a childlike state of fear and confusion and a world that is seen through the eyes of a child. The adult's capacity to deal with life does not exist for this part of the adult's mind. The childhood may be over, but a part of the adult never left.

The pain of being a child of one or more alcoholics teaches the child not to feel. If the child were to feel then the weight of his or her emotions would be too much to bear. Being helpless and subjected to inconsistent rules or even flat out abuse day in and day out cripples a young mind. The adult carries this emotional detachment forward.

As a child, it was a coping mechanism. It was a way to survive. As an adult, it keeps the person from moving on. It sabotages relationships of all kinds. Emotional distance is seen as necessary for survival even though it creates a limited existence.

You might think that you could merely tell the adult that the world is safe now, that there are no more reasons to be afraid and distant. The problem is that the parts of the adult's mind that need to hear this are not grown up. At this point, you are talking to a child.

People who do not have access to their emotions or who do not express them are likely to avoid the important conversations. They have learned to avoid the tough conversations and important topics because they could not do anything but make it worse when they were younger. This serves to sabotage relationships and to maintain the code of silence that was born in childhood. Never say what you feel. It will only make things worse. These phrases are mantras in the adult's mind. There is a good reason for this. They once helped to keep the child safe.

Depression or anxiety may be the product of living with alcoholic parents. The uncertainty and powerlessness of such an upbringing yields fear and hopelessness. These feelings create a view of the world as a dangerous place where one's circumstances cannot be changed. This learned helplessness makes for a dismal life.

These feelings pose a problem when they are brought into the present. The first experiences of intimacy were fraught with fear and mistrust that is brought into the relationships that follow. If not resolved then these issues can keep this adult from knowing true intimacy for a lifetime.

Adult children of alcoholics tend to share certain characteristics. Because they were brought up in such an unruly manner, they do not have a firm grasp on what normal behaviour is. They have never seen it in their own lives.

They have trouble following through on projects in general and may lie more out of habit than out of necessity. They tend to be overly critical of their own behaviour. Because they could not behave well enough as children to keep their parents from mistreating them, they continue to feel as though nothing they do is good enough.

As stated earlier, they have problems with intimacy and relationships. Because of their desire to control everything, they may have inappropriate emotional reactions to changes in general. In their minds, life is only safe if they are in control. If they are not in control they fear that bad things will happen as they did when they were a child.

They also seek approval to replace the approval that they did not receive as children. They never received it back then so they were not able to develop the internal belief that they were good enough. They seek approval in the present because they did not get it in the past.

The problem is that external approval is never enough to replace internal approval. Until the adult develops this internal feeling of being good enough then they will continue to seek it outside of themselves and will feel the effects of a childhood full of rejection if they ever do not receive this approval. The most basic act of rejection becomes too much to bear.

In addition to feeling not good enough, they often feel different than other people. They held the secrets of alcoholic parents as children and were always on the outside. They did not have anyone who could understand and bring this feeling of being an outsider with them everywhere they go.

This complicates the feeling of distance from others. This inexplicable feeling that one is different from and separate from the rest of the world may live on without requiring anything to sustain it in the present. The adult may never have a feeling of fitting in, of belonging, or of being loved. The secrets may be long gone but the feeling of a secret shame and a lack of love do not die so easily.

Adult children of alcoholics often exhibit loyalty to others to an extreme. This is problematic because these adults do not always offer this loyalty to those who deserve it. The necessary alliances that were forged with an alcoholic parent as children are mirrored in adulthood with similar undeserving parties receiving the loyalty. The drama of childhood is played out again and again with the same disastrous results.

Impulsivity is another consequence. These adults often engage in impulsive behaviors without a thought for the possible consequences. This can lead to further deterioration of self-esteem. The adult engages in shameful behaviors and does not feel the full repercussions until it is too late.

Adult children of alcoholics may not know why they feel the way they do or act the way they do. How could things that happened so long ago still be a driving force in anyone's life? The truth is that even when events are forgotten, the aftermath of those events can continue to dictate a person's entire life.

It may sound hopeless. The abuse and its echoes never end. This is only true when these events and the emotions that they created are never faced, dealt with, and released. The process for letting go of a childhood where a person had one or more alcoholic parents varies from person to person. Some individuals bounce back with a resilience that seems to come from nowhere. Others require professional help getting over the past.

It can be done. Having a childhood with one or more alcoholic parents does not doom you to a lifetime of emotional distance and confusing emotions being triggered at every turn. The goal of realizing all the possible consequences of such a childhood is not to foster a feeling of powerlessness but of hope. It is in the awareness of the underlying mechanisms of dysfunction that it can be undone.

Silence was a large part of the problem for children who grew up in an alcoholic home. Feelings were not expressed. They were covered up by alcohol and then buried in shame and fear. It is in the uncovering and open recognition of these feelings that truths of the past can be spoken.

When these truths are spoken, they lose their power. Their power resides in their silence, in the shame and fear that protect them. Their power can be taken away. A painful past can be healed. Looking at what was wrong with the past helps you to realize what must be done to make the present right.

Protecting Children From The Consequences Of Alcohol Abuse

If you have children in the home, you must protect them from alcohol abuse. These means that they have to be protected from the alcohol and the alcoholic that may be abusive. Kids are very impressionable and learn from what they see or what is done to them. You have to be the one to break the cycle. If you do not protect the children from the abuse no matter if it is physical or because they see a parent drinking, they could grow up with the same tendencies. As a parent or even a friend, you must step in and prevent any problems before they start.

Kids will follow in the footsteps of a parent if they do not understand the consequences. This is not always true, but in most cases, it is what happens. Even if a child does not take after the parent, they may grow up to accept this type of behavior and put their own lives in danger or have nothing but heartache. You have to protect the children so that they know that this is not the way to live. However, sometimes this can be hard to do if you want to remain in the home.

If there is abuse in the home because of alcohol, you need to shield the kids from this abuse. If the abuse is physical, mental or verbal, kids should not have to live with it. it the abuse is watching their parent drink themselves into a drunken state, they need to know that this is not how people should live. As a parent, you have to make a decision whether to stay or take you children somewhere else where they will not be subjected to the abusive behavior or have to watch mom or dad drink themselves to death.

Never tell the kids that drinking is just something you do. It is not something that you just do. They need to understand that alcoholism is a disease that can have devastating effects on the person doing the drinking as well as the family. This is important for children to understand. This does not mean that telling them that their parent is a loser or a bad person. You have to be truthful without being demeaning to the parent with the problem. Children are smart and will know that other families do live as you do.

You may need to leave the home for a while if the drinking leads to abusive behavior. This is the only way to protect the children and make sure that they do not grow up thinking that this is acceptable behavior. You also do not want to keep them in an abusive home. Not all alcoholics drink all the time, but even so, the kids should not be subjected to any abusive behavior from a parent. They also should be told that drinking is all right. As they grow up, they would stand a good chance of following in the footsteps of the alcoholic parent.

Take the kids to Al-Anon so that they have someone other than you to talk with. This is very important so that the kids have someone to talk to and listen to other kids in the same situation. If they have somewhere to go with others their age, it could help them understand what is happening and how to cope with their home life. It can also help them understand if you have to leave the home.

Talk with the kids if they have questions. You have to be honest without being judgemental. The kids will understand more if you talk to them instead of trying to hide the problem. Kids today, know more than what parents knew when they were kids and they see and hear things that they probably should not. This is the reason that you must be honest. Never badmouth the alcoholic parent because the kids could resent you.

When you are talking to the kids, ask them if they have questions and try to answer them the best you can. You can also expect to be asked why mom or dad yells at them or why the person has to do the things that he or she does. Answer honestly and try to help them understand.

Talking To Children About The Alcoholic Parent

Living with an alcoholic is even more difficult when you have kids that are seeing this display. It is hard to explain to kids why one parent has to drink and not do anything with the family. In many cases, kids ask questions that need to be answered and you have a hard time doing it. You do not want them to hate the parent that drinks, but you also do not want them to follow in the same footsteps. They also might not want to have friends over because of the drinking. As a parent, you have to talk to the kids so that they understand.

Be honest with the kids. If they have questions, you have to give them truthful answers. You do not have to say that the parent is a drunk, but you do have to explain that drinking is a disease and the parent needs help, but is not getting it. Explaining and answering their questions can be hard. Sometimes you just want to tell them that you do not know why the person drinks, but then you are not helping them understand anything. You need to be truthful, but you also have to shield them from some things about the alcoholic.

They have friends and they do not want their friends to see a drunken parent. This can be very hard for kids to understand. This is especially hard on the kids if the other kid's parents are the ones forbidding the kids to come to your house. Many parents do not want their kids subjected to the problems or the alcohol abuse. They are afraid of what might happen. This hard for the kids and when the other kids cannot come and play at their house, they can become lonely and depressed.

You have to be strong for the kids, but you also need to make sure that they have a good life. This can be done by being there for them and taking them to places where they will have fun with other kids. Sometimes it is easier to let the kids play at the neighbor's house so they are not around the drinking, but then they are not getting the attention they need from the non-drinking parent. It is hard to have kids in a home where an alcoholic resides.

Ask them how they feel and listen. You need to understand how the kids feel. They have no one to talk to but you. It is not like they can discuss their feelings with their friends. You have to be there for them and listen to how they feel. It is not uncommon for children of alcoholic parents to grow up to drink. They are learning at a young age that drinking is acceptable unless you tell them differently.

Make sure that the kids understand that this is not how people should live. You have to stress the unhealthiness of drinking. You are the teacher and you have to make sure that the kids do not grow up thinking that this way of living is all there is for them. If you need help talking to a child, support groups and even a church minister can help. Children of alcoholic parents need to have some structure in their life outside of the home. You have to make sure that the kids are happy and well cared for so that they grow up to be well-adjusted adults even if you live with an alcoholic.

V.

LIVING WITH ALCOHOLISM

So all this is good to know, but how do you cope while you are living this existence? How do you live your daily life with an alcoholic in that life? Is there any way to make the days bearable?

You need to realize that the situation is not your fault. You further need to realize that you do not have control over the situation. You can try to help, but it is up to the alcoholic to accept the help. You do what you can and after that you have to let go of it. You cannot always change the way things are. You need to focus on what you can do and on your life.

This point cannot be overemphasized. The problem is not your fault. Its continuation is not your fault. Nothing that you did or said or did not do or did not say created this problem. Do not blame yourself. Blaming yourself only creates feelings of guilt. This is not a problem that you created, and it is not one that you can solve. You can offer help, but that is it.

Not blaming yourself can be made even harder if the alcoholic in your life blames you. This can happen. In searching for someone to blame, the alcoholic is likely to choose someone close, and that someone might be you.

While it may make you feel like you are at fault, the alcoholic in your life is confused and in pain. They are looking for someone else to blame and you being close only makes it convenient. It does not make it true. You cannot cause alcoholism no matter what you do. It is a far more complex disease than anything you could singlehandedly create.

To begin with, you can confront the alcoholic in your life. You can tell them what you are seeing, how their drinking is affecting you, and how that makes you feel. You may wish to talk to them one on one or plan an intervention with friends and family members. It all depends on how far the problem has progressed and what you feel is right.

There is no single right way to handle the situation. You may want to get some advice from a therapist or visit a group such as Al-Anon. They will be able to give you insight into your unique situation. Each case is different and will have its own complications. Someone who has experience with this predicament will be able to help you choose a course of action and will be able to prepare you for what might happen. You will want to know as much as you can going into this situation.

Remember, you can make the effort, but you cannot make it turn out the way you want. This is one instance where you need to let go of the outcome and accept that there are some things you cannot control. This is one of them.

So what else can you do? The list of things you cannot do seems to include all the things you most want to accomplish. The things that you can do are just as important even if they do not seem to be.

Take care of yourself. This is the most important thing. This is the one area where you really do have control. You do not want your life, your health, and your happiness to become lost in the trials of having an alcoholic in your life.

You cannot help someone else into a healthier life if you are not living one. You need interests and friends that are separate from and untouched by the alcoholic influence. This will help you to retain a healthy view of the world. The world of the alcoholic is distorted. You do not need to live your life in a distorted world too.

Begin with the basics. Eat healthy foods, get plenty of sleep, and enjoy yourself. Find fun activities that you can participate in. Take up a hobby, or join a bowling league. Do whatever it takes to remind yourself that life is full of joy. Get enough exercise too. This will release endorphins to help you deal with stress and provides a wonderful physical release.

Your new healthier lifestyle will often affect those around you and inspire them to make healthy changes too. The simple things are what you have to remember when you are trying to keep your life healthy in the midst of an unhealthy influence. You need to create a healthy life and make healthy choices not only for yourself but for those around you.

Do not play the role of a victim. You may be faced with the alcoholic, drunk or not, accusing you, berating you, or trying to reason with you. It is at this point that you need to realize that you cannot win an argument with an inebriated person. Even if the person is sober at the moment then arguing with that person is often fruitless.

Do not fall into unproductive patterns. You cannot argue with an addiction. Do not even try.

Handling The Responsibilities Alone

When you live with an alcoholic, you not only feel alone, but most of the time you really are when it comes to chores and the kids. You are the only adult in the home it feels like most of the time. You will not be able to rest until all the work around the house is done and if you want to go somewhere, you will take the kids with you because the other parent will not be able to care for them while he or she is drinking. You might even have to have a job on top of everything else.

You will have to make sure the bills are paid on time. You will also need to make sure that the family has enough money for everything after the alcohol is bought out of the family budget. You may have to get a job just to survive and pay the bills. This could be the hardest thing you have to do in your life, especially if you thought that your spouse or partner was going to take care of the work and you were going to take care of the house and the family. Things change when the alcohol consumes one of the partners.

You will usually have to clean and take out the garbage. This is just because it will at least get done the right way. He or she may want to do dishes, but when you try to do something when you are drunk, it usually backfires. Dirty dishes in the cupboards that are said to be clean can be disturbing. Taking out the garbage can also be a challenge and if you want everything to be taken out, then you will probably have to do it yourself. You can plan on doing almost everything around the house including cleaning up messes that he or she may make.

The person may not want supper when you do, so you will have to make sure that there is enough food leftover for them. This is something that can cause arguments. If dinner is not just right, it can trigger an argument. You will never win, so you always do what is asked of you, even if it means making something new. This can get old fast and make you wish that you were the one drinking. Just do not ever give up hope.

You will have to secretly keep a hold on the money and know where it is going. An alcoholic in your life means that money is going to be tight because they will always have money for alcohol, but may not have enough for anything else. If you want to keep your home and have things for the family including food, you need to take control of the money. Even if they say no, you must find a way to do it.

The kids will be your responsibility and you will need to keep them in line by yourself. You can pretty much figure that anything that requires the attention of a parent is going to be your responsibility. In some cases, you will even hear that you were the one that had kids. It can be hard on the kids just as much as it is on you. Kids need both parents for support and most of the time, they do not have this when one parent is an alcoholic. Living with an alcoholic can be challenging and devastating to kids and to you.

Life With An Alcoholic May Not Be Possible

If you have lived with an alcoholic for years and feel despair, you may need a change. No one should live without love and happiness. Sometimes it is not possible to stay with the alcoholic because you feel alone and helpless. You need something more in your life and the person is not able to give you what you need. Everyone needs to feel love and sometimes the person that you thought was the love of your life turns out to be your worst nightmare, literally. Sometimes life with an alcoholic is not possible and you may have to leave.

Sometimes, you just have to leave and try to get over him or her. This can be hard, but after the years of living the way you have been makes it a little easier. You may move out temporarily or permanently. Maybe you think that the person will change if you leave and they have to live on their own. You think that they do not need you anyways so they will probably not even care. This is the hardest feeling to live with for anyone. You may still care, but you do not believe that the person you are leaving does.

They want the alcohol more than they want you. This is hard to accept. You wonder why they would choose drinking over you. The truth hurts and you have to accept that you cannot help the person. No matter what you do, they always seem to find their way back to a bottle. You have to move on if you want a loving relationship. Then they do something that makes you feel all warm inside. They stop drinking for a while and things are wonderful until it starts again. Now, you have to start thinking about leaving all over again.

The hardest thing to do is leave someone that you love, but you have to sometimes. Even if they are wonderful for a time to keep you there with them, you still have to make a change. You have to think about yourself and make decisions that can be hard. The hardest part of living with an alcoholic is leaving them for their own good and yours. Sometimes it is hard to be strong, but you need all the courage you can find to say good-bye. You have to stand tall and have confidence in yourself, which you lost somewhere down the line.

You have to think about yourself. You cannot continue to live in fear or without a partner. You need love. You need companionship. You need to be free from the alcoholism. Even if you are not a drinker, you are affected by the drinking. Sometimes an alcoholic affects you more than the alcohol affects him or her. Even if you are not battered or abused, you are because the alcohol wins. You feel defeated by a bottle.

You lose years of being loved. However, you need to grow old with someone that can love you and cuddle you. You need someone that turns to you and not to a bottle. Living with an alcoholic is not easy and you grow tired of being the only one in the relationship that tries. The only choice you have is to leave and start new. You have to break free of the alcoholic and start a new life with someone that does not need alcohol to live. You need stability in your life for the first time in a long time.

Finding Support

Finding support is essential to deal with a situation as trying as living with an alcoholic. You will need help dealing with all that comes up. Finding support begins with having friends and family around you who will be there for whatever you need. You need to know that you are not alone.

It is easy to get caught up in the problems of an alcoholic and to make that your entire world. Create your own support network of family friends. Know what you can get from them. Some may be close enough to be available at all hours while others may be able to be there if you need someone to listen. Give others a chance to help out with whatever you need.

They will not be able to help with everything. Those who have not lived through the experience of living with or dealing with an alcoholic will only be able to help to a degree. They will not understand the daily trials, the emotions, or the overall experience that you are currently living. For this type of insight and understanding you will have to turn to those who have been through these circumstances. The best place to turn to for this level of understanding is Al-Anon.

The Al-Anon Organization

Al-Anon is an organization that has existed for over 55 years. It offers a place for the friends and families of alcoholics to come together to share their common experiences. You may need a little extra support, or you may be feeling utterly hopeless about the situation. This is the place to go to find those who have been through or who are going through what you are going through.

Al-Anon exists for all those who need help dealing with being a friend or family member of an alcoholic. It does not matter if the problem is just beginning, is in its worst stages, or is beginning to heal. Those at all stages of the process are welcome because everyone has insight to share. At the very least, this is the place to come to feel that you are not alone. Alcoholism is more common than you would think. You really are not alone.

It is not a place just to reflect on the problems of living with an alcoholic in your life. Al-Anon is a place where you can share what has worked and what has not. You can share what has happened, the signs you have seen, and what has helped. You can share what you are going through and have your feelings understood.

You can learn ways of helping the alcoholic in your life and, most importantly, ways of helping yourself. You can learn that your happiness is not dependent upon anyone but you. You do not need someone else to give up alcohol to be happy. You do not want alcoholism to steal your life as it is stealing the life of your loved one.

You are not required to speak during meetings. You may not feel comfortable sharing your story. That is fine. You can sit and listen to learn from the experiences of others. You can also receive literature that may help to answer your questions and cement your newfound understanding that you are not alone in this.

Everything that happens at Al-Anon meetings is anonymous. Nothing you say will be repeated outside of the meetings so you can feel free to share all that you wish. You do not have to share but you always have the option.

You do not need to pay any fees to attend Al-Anon meetings. Members can donate whatever they wish to maintain the basic costs of running such a group, but you are under no obligation to contribute.

You need to be able to provide support for yourself. Disentangling yourself from the patterns brought about by the alcoholic in your life may be difficult, but you have to do it if you want to be happy. You have to maintain parts of life that are untouched by alcoholism. This means you need your own hobbies, activities, interests, and friends who are not affected by alcoholism.

It is easy to forget what a normal life is when you live with someone whose behavior is far from normal. The subtle, slow changes that turn your life from a typical life to one warped by alcoholism can distort your view of reality. You cannot help someone with alcoholism if you give in to the distortions created by the disease. If you stay around this influence all the time and repeat the patterns that the disease began then you are helping to keep the disease going.

Your happiness and your mental health are about more than helping the alcoholic in your life. Alcoholism may put its stamp on large parts of your life, but you should not have to trade in your happiness to stand by someone you love.

As big as their problem is, it is yours too. You need support, encouragement, untainted love, and joy in life. As much as you want to and should separate yourself from this problem, it is your problem too. When you have an alcoholic in your life then you need help. Somehow you became ingrained in patterns that alcoholism formed, and you need to find a way out of these patterns.

Help your loved one as much as you can, create boundaries so that this help does not rob you of your life, and always take care of yourself first. It does not help anyone to sacrifice your life over something you cannot control. Maintain your own happiness and when they are ready, your loved one will join you in that happiness.

The Support Of Family And Friends

You do not have to go it alone. You can join a support group and talk with family and friends about what you are living with. It is important that you are not alone in what you are living with. If you think that it will make people feel differently about the person, you may be right, but then again, the alcoholic does not care anyway. You need to have someone to talk to or confide in if you do not join a support group. You would be surprised at how many friends and family already know that there is a problem.

Talk to your family about the problem. You need the support of your family to make it when you live with an alcoholic. They can offer advice and support, but also they will know what you are going through. Some of your family made be understanding sand some may be a bit skeptic about the problem. It is not unusual for family members to be in denial as much as the alcoholic is if they think that he or she is the greatest. You still need to let everyone know what is happening.

Talk to your friends about the problem. Many times a friend can see things that you cannot. Sometimes they already know, but did not want to say anything until you brought it up for conversations. If you do talk with friends, you have to make sure that they are not going to gossip about the situation, which could make matters worse. You can talk to close friends that understand. Maybe they have even been in the same situation. This can help you more than you think. If you do not or cannot join a group, the friends and family are the next best thing to have supporting you.

Talk to his or her family about the problem only if you feel that they care about it. The same goes for his or her friends. Since you can talk to your friends and family, it would be nice if you could talk to his or her family. This can be a touchy area, as most families do not want to admit that their family member has a drinking problem. If you can find just one member of the family or just one friend, you can talk to them for help and support. Sometimes they can help by talking to the family member when you are not around.

You need to have family and friends that can support you if you want to live with an alcoholic. This is the only way that you will be able to stay sane. If you have an abusive relationship when the person is drinking, you need to have someone that knows what is going on in your home. It is always better to talk to a support group, but for some reason, that might not be an option for you. They may even be able to help you if you need to get away for a while and breathe easy for a few days.

Be open and honest. If things are not good, explain this and ask for suggestions. Many times, it is easier to hide behind the scenes and not say anything. Unfortunately, this is not a good idea. If you live with an alcoholic, you have to have support and someone that knows what you are going through. This is important if something would happen to you or the alcoholic. Even if you think that nothing could ever happen, you are wrong. Someone that drinks and for long periods, does not always think rationally or even know what they do.

Never ask a family or friend to talk to the alcoholic unless they know the person better than you do. This could make him or her upset with you, but it might help if they have a respect for that person. Living with an alcoholic is not easy and you will find times that you even make mistakes, but you are only trying to help and some day he or she may be able to see that.

Join A Co-Dependency Group

If you are co-dependent on an alcoholic, you may need to join a co-dependency group for help. Living with an alcoholic can be hard, but when you feel that you need to stay for one reason or another, it makes things even harder than they already are for you. There are groups for co-dependent friends or family members. These groups can help you understand why you need this person and what you might be able to do about it. If you think you are co-dependent, you will want to find a group that can help you so that you understand why you need this person.

They offer you the support you need. It is easier to sit in a group and hear others talk. When you do, you might learn a few things about yourself. You may find out that you really care about this person or you might find out that this person has control over you in a way that is not healthy to you. If you have kids or even if you don't, you will want to find out why you stay and if it for a good reason or a bad reason. No one makes you do anything you do not want to do. They are there to help and listen.

If you want to leave the alcoholic, you need to learn why you stay first. Before you can get up and leave an alcoholic, you need to know why you stay. It might be that you stay because you deeply care about this person and want to help them. Living with an alcoholic can be hard, but if you have love for that person, it can be harder to live with. If you want to leave that person, you have to know why you stayed or hooked up with that person in the first place.

You need to understand why the person has control over you. If you stay with an alcoholic and you have no reason why or it is because you are afraid to be on your own, you need to know how this happened. Is this person controlling you? Is this person verbally abusing you and lowering your self-esteem? Is this person physically abusing you? Do you stay because you are afraid to leave for fear of what will happen? The co-dependency group can help you understand. You need to understand why you stay before you can understand yourself.

When you understand why you stay, you can then begin to help yourself. This is the only way to either live with an alcoholic or leave that person. The co-dependency group offers the support you need to talk about why you stay and what your own fears are. This group is a good way to find yourself. If you have been abused, this group can offer support and advice. You need to have someone to talk to about the problems that you live with every day.

The co-dependency group can help you in more ways that you think. When you attend a group, you will hear other people's stories. You may even hear your story from someone else's mouth. You are not alone. There is help for those that live with alcoholics. There are ways to take control of your life and help the other person as well. If you have children, it is especially important that you understand if you have a co-dependency issue.

If you are living with an alcoholic and you do not understand why you stay, you may need to attend a support group for co-dependency. You may not even realize why you stay. You have to understand yourself before you can understand what is happening to you. If you have children, you have to think about them as well as yourself. Maybe you need to take time away from the alcoholic to figure out what keeps you with that person. The co-dependency group can help you resolve any issues you might have before it is too late. Then again, you have to think about everyone concerned.

Daily Living Management Tips

Give Love & Conversation When Sober

If you live with an alcoholic, you want to offer love and conversation when they are not drinking. Trying this when they are drinking may be harder to do since you never know what their mood is or how they will react. You have to have an open line of communication even if the person is an alcoholic. You should not try talking about anything important when they are drinking, but engage is light conversation and leave the heavy discussions for when they are sober. Then you can have a friendly conversation. Just show them some love and hope that they like that better than what they get when they drink.

If the alcoholic is not a mean drunk, you can offer love. This of course depends on the mood of the alcoholic when he is drinking. Some alcoholics are mellow drunks, but even the mildest mannered alcoholic can switch moods just like that without warning. It can be like a roller coaster. One minute they can be sweet and loving and the next screaming at you because you said something that they did not like. This is a pattern with most alcoholics. You never know what you can say or do. It can change from day to day or even minute to minute.

When the alcoholic is not drinking, engage in conversation and try to touch on the drinking. This is the only time you have to discuss drinking. In most cases, they will tell you that they do not have a problem. They do not see it the same way that you do. You could point out a few things that they do when they drink and hope that they remember. You can tell them how it makes you feel when they have to drink all the time. It probably will not help them, but it can help you.

Explain that you want to care about them and do not want to see something bad happen. You can pour out your feelings and at least let them know how you feel, but chances are, they will only quick drinking for a few days and then start hiding it from you. This is common with alcoholics. If they know that you do not want them to drink, they will find ways to do it and hide it. It would not be uncommon to find empties in cupboards, down in the basement or out in the garage.

Talk about the future and things you would like to do. Make it clear that you want to enjoy a life with them, but you want them to be around for it. Make it clear that you are not really happy with the ways things are, but you would like to help make a change. Never tell them that they have to change, make it a change for both of you. You may not need to change, but telling them that is not going to mean a thing. You have to tell them that you will change with them.

Explain some of the health risks that you discovered. This may be one thing that could help. If they do not want to die at a young age, they may think about what you have to say. Of course, if they do not feel as if they have a problem, you could be talking to deaf ears. You can still try. Maybe if they see or feel some symptoms, they will think about what you said.

Try not to get upset or yell. Engage in a light conversation and if you feel yourself getting upset, take a moment to collect your thoughts. The last thing the alcoholic wants to do is listen to you yell at them. If you do not walk away and calm down, they might just leave and find somewhere to drink. This will defeat the purpose of your talk. You have to be on eggshells when you live with an alcoholic if you want to help them. You can be caring when you talk, but do not expect that in return from the alcoholic. That may come over time.

Avoid Alcohol Related Arguments

Alcohol and arguing just do not mix. In some cases, a minor argument can escalate into something much worst. The slightest comment can set off a full-blown fight. Sometimes the fights can end badly for both. It is not uncommon for fights to erupt in the household when you live with an alcoholic. Even the sweetest person can become mean if they feel threatened in any way. The only way to avoid any arguments from escalating is to avoid any arguments or discussions when the person is under the influence. This might be hard to do, but it is something that you have to do.

Making the most of a bad situation is hard to do, but you must try. You might have to walk away even though you know that you are right about something. You have to avoid making things worst. If the person drinking feels strongly that they are right or that you did something wrong, they are not going to see it any different by arguing with them. They are going to get angrier and this is when physical, verbal and mental abuse can occur. This can be the hardest part of living with an alcoholic. However, to avoid serious problems, you should drop it and walk away.

If the arguing starts, you should leave the room and not say another word. If you continue to argue, you are just adding to the fire. This is when bad things can happen. The alcoholic that believes that they are right and that you are the wrong one, they could fight back if you continue to talk. It is not uncommon to hear how bad you are or how they detest the sight of you. You have to walk away before this starts. Even if you leave the room, the yelling may continue, but at least you will be out of harm's way.

Make sure that you are not starting the arguments when they start. This is the worst thing you can do. If you know the person is drinking and had enough, talking about anything could set them off. This is not the time to talk about no money for food or the car needs repair. You will just start an argument that you will not win. The alcoholic never loses the fight because they never back down in most cases. They are not thinking clearly and have no idea what is what.

Make sure that the kids know that this not the time to discuss anything with the alcoholic adult. Kids should never discuss anything with the parent who is drinking. Even the sweetest parent can become the meanest person when they are drinking. You never know what will set them off or what they will do. They are under the influence of a mind-altering addiction. Always wait until they are not drinking before letting the kids talk to the drinking parent.

If the argument continues after you leave the room, you may have to leave the house for a while. This is sad, but it is the truth in some cases. They may follow you around yelling at you. You may need to leave for a while so that they can calm down. If you do, make sure to take the kids and the car keys for all cars. Give them a few hours to calm down before returning. Sometimes, it is better to wait until they pass out. Just avoid any confrontations when the person is drinking. It is much safer for you.

Never Accuse The Alcoholic Of Being An Alcoholic

If you live with someone that drinks, the last thing you should do is accuse him or her of being an alcoholic. Not only will you lose the debate, but they will become upset and in some cases, verbally, physically or mentally abusive. An alcoholic has to be the one to admit that they have a problem and there is no one else that can tell them any different. They will not listen to you no matter what you say. You might mention that the drinking is getting out of hand, but they may not think that there is a problem.

A never-ending fight is all you will have. If you accuse the alcoholic of drinking too much, they will defend themselves to no avail. They will insist that it is you that has problems and whatever else they can think of to say. You will never win the battle in this case. If you live with an alcoholic, you will need a support group such an Al-Anon to help you. You need to talk with others that are going through the same thing as you. The problems will not go away until the alcoholic decides that they have a problem.

They can make you believe that they have not been drinking and they even believe it. This is common when you live with an alcoholic. They can hide their drinking because you accuse them of drinking. Then when you accuse them of drinking or you find the empties, they will tell you that those are from months ago, even though you know better. The horrible truth is that the alcoholic believes what he or she is saying to you and can sound so convincing. This is how they make you doubt yourself.

You will only start an argument if you continue to accuse him or her of being an alcoholic. This is a problem for anyone that lives with an alcoholic. You want to make them see what they are doing, but all you will succeed in doing is making them defensive and lie more. When the person is not drinking, you could mention the problem, but chances are they are going to deny any wrong doings. They can be very secretive and deceitful when it comes to drinking. They will do anything to drink and you will not stop them.

They will not want to hear what you have to say even when they are sober. An alcoholic that thinks that they do not have a problem may not listen to you even when they are sober. They are sober so how could they have a problem. They can make you feel as if you are imaging a problem or even looking for reasons to start a fight. You will never win. However, you cannot let this fool you. You know there is a problem and you have to keep on top of everything.

There will come a day, when they will do something that will make them think about their drinking. Unfortunately, they will only be good for a short time. If they break something or hurt you, they will be sorry and make promises. Unfortunately, this is only a short-term fix. They are not going to stop drinking. They may slow down for a while until the urge takes over again. Then it will be back to the same thing all over again until the next time.

Dealing With Rejection

An alcoholic can push the person that loves them away. They only need the alcohol and not you. They can become distant and cold. If you love this person, it can be hard to live with or accept. You have to watch the person move farther away from you while you sit and watch. Soon, you are so far back in line that you feel as if you are all alone with no one in your life. This can happen to even the most loving couples. Alcohol does something to the brain and the body that changes a person. They withdrawal from reality and live in their own little world without you.

Never force yourself on the alcoholic if they do not want to be close to you. If the person you love does not want you, there is nothing you can do to change it. The person is not going to change their mind just because you are trying to make things work. You should never try to be with an alcoholic that does not want anything to do with you. This can anger them and makes things unpleasant for both of you. You have to keep your distance and if they want you near, they will tell you. The hardest part is waiting.

Ask for help from a counsellor or from a support group. You will start to feel all alone and you need help accepting what is happening to your relationship. Support groups can help you talk things through before you start to doubt yourself. There are people that have experienced the same thing and can help you. They can tell you how it affected them and learn what they did to cope. You can talk about anything because the group is there for you and everyone else. There is always someone that is experiencing the same thing that you are or they have in the past.

Do not feel as if it is your fault that the alcoholic does not want you. Yes, you may have changed, but you have to change when you live with an alcoholic. You are not any less lovable, it is the person that chooses to drink that makes the decisions and you cannot change his or her mind. Just because one person does not want you does not mean that you are any less the person you were when you first met. Alcohol affects a person's way of thinking and usually it alters the way of thinking.

You can live together in a home without any contact if that is how you want to live. This is a horrible way to live especially if you are starved for love and affection. It is very possible to co-exist in one home and never have any contact with each other. If you want an alcoholic roommate, this is what you will have. There are not many people that can live like this and be happy. You will still have the aggravation associated with living with an alcoholic, but you just will not be able to help.

Try to talk to him or her when the time is right. See if there is any hope of establishing a new relationship. See if the person wants a relationship. Most alcoholics do not care for anyone but themselves. All they need is alcohol and maybe a place to sleep. They do not need a bed companion or a housekeeper. They really do not need anyone. You have to adjust or live with the feelings of loneliness. You have a hard decision to make if you stay in the relationship.

If you have kids, it makes it harder. You want the kids to have both parents, but if the parent that is drinking does not want to be a part of the kid's life, they will suffer as well. Kids are impressionable and need stability with one or two parents rather than with one parent and one that does not want anything to do with them. You have to think about the kids and yourself. You have to know what is important to everyone.

Dealing With The Cycle Of Insincerity & Uncertainty

When you live with an alcoholic that always apologizes for hurting you, eventually the apologies do not mean much. If the person continues to do the things that they keep saying their sorry for, you have to wonder if they ever meant one word of the apology. This is a common feeling. You can only listen to apologies so many times before you start to think that it is a programmed response that has no meaning. Alcoholics are great at saying that they are sorry, but they have a hard time not doing the same thing again. When you love someone, this is hard to understand.

The first time something happens, they will be sorry the next day. This is because they have sober up and more than likely, they have a memory of what they have done or you have told them. They will be sweet and apologetic because they truly are sorry. However, they can promise it will never happen again, but when they drink, they have no control over what they do. It can happen again. This time it might be a little worst then the first time. After the first time, you felt content to believe them, but if it happens again, you have to think about whether or not they really meant it.

Once it happens again, and they say they are sorry, you have to start wondering when it will happen again and again. This is the hardest part of living with an alcoholic. You never know for sure if they mean anything that they say. You start to doubt their love for you and wonder why they never lash out at anyone else. Sometimes they do, but it is rare for an alcoholic to just go off on someone that did not provoke them, accept you.

Then you start to wonder if they will ever say they are sorry and mean it. This is the worst feeling in the world. You are doubting their sincerity and you start to doubt other things that they say to you including that fact that they love you. You start to think how they could do this to you repeatedly if they did love you. Now, you not only live with an alcoholic, you live with the doubt. This can eat away at you to no end. This is when the trust starts to fade.

After years of hearing sorry, you just do not believe them anymore. You doubt every word they say to you and you cannot believe anything that they say to you. The home is no longer a home. It turns into a prison that you made for yourself. You now have more confusion and do not know what to do. You still care for the person, but you wonder if you could ever love that person again. The times of happiness are gone and all you are left with is drinking and broken promises.

You lose all hope and feel all alone. You want to leave, but you feel as if you owe the person something. You can become withdrawn and hopeless. You may even wonder why you should be the only responsible and sober person in the home. You start to feel all alone with no one to turn to for help. You look for answers, but you find emptiness. You wonder what to do next. Your life has not turned out as you expected it to when you first met the person and you need happiness to live. You turn to someone else or you turn to the same demon that took the love from you.

Dealing With The Frustration & Hopelessness

When you live with an alcoholic in your life, it is hard not to get discouraged and just want to walk away. If you care about the person, you want to help them, but the truth is that they are the only one that can take the first steps to helping him to herself. You can try to help as much as possible and do things to make things easier to quit, but sometimes all the help and treatments in the world are not enough. You have to be positive and hope that the day will come when the person finally goes for treatment and wins the battle of alcoholism.

Remember why you fell in love with the person. This is important or you will not make it. Many times, you will hate the person and other times, you will see a part of them come shining through.

It is even harder when you live with an alcoholic that drinks and becomes mean and then goes a couple days of being their same loving self. They become the person you fell in love with. However, it can end in a minute when they start drinking again. This is the hardest thing to live with.

Think about the person they used to be and how much fun you used to have. This can work for a time, but after years of abusing alcohol, it can be hard to think about the good times. The person that lives with an alcoholic needs to be strong. This can be hard for some people, but if you love the person, you have to try. It is hard to watch them do this to themselves, but you have to give them love anyway. It is possible to make a difference if you remain strong.

Remember that there is help for you and the alcoholic. There are groups that offer support to the spouse or family of the alcoholic. Al-Anon is a great group to join. You can hear others talk and can even relate to what they are saying. After all, you are living the same nightmare that most of them are living. You have to have support to make it through the hard times. This is vital to living with an alcoholic. The support should come from family and friends as well. If the family does not have a clue as to what is happening, they cannot offer support.

Look at picture albums and see the joyous times you shared. This is a mask of the problem, but it does help. You see the times when the drinking did not control your life. You see another person standing next to you. Browsing through picture albums with the sober alcoholic may bring back memories for him or her as well. Sometimes it is these times that they start to think about what they are doing and want a change.

If you are living with an alcoholic, you have to stand up and let them know that you are feeling alone. You have to let them know that you are there for them, but they are the ones that have to change. You cannot do it for them, but you can offer support and encouragement if they agree to treatment. You are part of the process, but the person that drinks is the only one that can make things better.

Helping Your Alcoholic Child

When you are dealing with an alcoholic child, you have to be firm and not think that things will change. You cannot think that this is just a phase that they are going through. Many parents prefer to think that their child young or old is just having a rough time and just needs to unwind. This is what can lead to alcohol abuse and future problems. Someone that drinks because they need to unwind or because the parent thinks it is just a phase can become an alcoholic if this type of behavior continues. Parents never want to believe that their child has a drinking problem.

If your child is an alcoholic, you need to understand that sticking up for them when they do something wrong is not going to help them. If they are a younger child or an adult child with a family, you as a parent cannot allow them to continue doing the things that they do. You have to be responsible enough to see that there is a problem and take steps to help. Making excuses or believing that your child could never do something bad is wrong. You do not know for certain what they are capable of doing when they are drinking.

No matter if is an adult child or a young child, you need to be firm and not coddle them. A parent that sees nothing and does not want to know anything is just asking for trouble. Coddling a child that is an alcoholic can show them that what they are doing is acceptable. This could lead to something horrible happening. If you believe that your child could never be abusive or that they have a drinking problem, you are just enabling them to continue. Waking up one day to find out that your child has hurt someone or his or her self can be devastating.

It was probably coddling that got them into the mess they are in now. If you wear blinders where your children are concerned, it is more than likely going to be your fault if something happens. If you know that there is a drinking problem, you must be strong. Allowing your child to drink in excess can lead to repercussions. As a parent of an alcoholic child, young or old, you must deal with the problem instead of coddling them and making excuses for them.

If a spouse or partner tells you that your son or daughter has a drinking problem, never blame the spouse or partner. They are not the ones who are drinking. Alcoholics do not need a reason to drink. They drink because they have a disease and an addiction that they need help overcoming. By turning a blind eye to the problem, you are making matters worse. If a spouse tells you that your child has a drinking problem and is abusive at times, tell that person that it is their fault is not going to help your child.

Parents do not want to hear that their child is an alcoholic. No parent wants to hear this, but the facts are that any child from any background can have a drinking problem. If you as a parent do not address the problem, you are enabling your child to continue drinking and endangering anyone around them including yourself. You must help and be supportive of the spouse and your child, but you cannot deny there is a problem. You as a parent have to take steps to get your child help.

Living With The Lies & Deceit

Living with an alcoholic can be hard enough with the drinking, but if the alcoholic also lies and is deceitful, it can makes things worst. You have to wonder which part of the conversation is a lie and which part is the truth. You may find out things that you wish you never heard, but the truth is that an alcoholic can lie and not even bat an eyelash. Not all alcoholics are deceitful and lie, but most are at some point in their lives. You really have to be strong to live with an alcoholic. You have to be in love to go through all of the problems that come with an alcoholic.

The lies can hurt more than the alcohol addiction. This depends on the type of lies, but if it is about relationships, you can become bitter and may even want to leave the person. The alcoholic can lie about money, work, other relationships or just about every day happenings. You are left behind when the alcoholic lies and tries to hide things from you. The sad thing about this is that you always find out about the lies and when you confront them, they act as if you have loss your mind. In most cases, this is exactly how you feel.

The deceit is something that the alcoholic is good at doing. They can tell you one thing and be doing another. They always feel that they are right and you are wrong. What they do is not deceitful because they are not doing anything wrong. After you live like for a few years, you begin to wonder why you live like this. You want answers, but chances are the answer would be a lie anyway. After time, the alcoholic has told so many lies that he or she honestly believes the lies and the truth fades into the background.

Sometimes the person will steal if they need money for a drink. This is a problem for any family. There always seems that the money goes fast enough without having someone take it for alcohol. You have to keep your money safe and place somewhere where no one but you knows where it is when you need it. This way of living is not healthy, but if you want to live with the alcoholic, you have to keep the money safe.

You have to make your own decisions whether to stay or leave. With all the lies and deceit, you can become withdrawn and start to doubt yourself. You wonder about your self-worth. Your self-esteem is affected. You wonder if this is all your life is going to be. Are you just on this earth to live with a person that drinks, steals and lies? You need someone to talk to that can reassure you that you are a great person. The person that lives with the alcoholic can become very depressed because of the lies and deceit.

You need to have someone to talk to so that you do not feel alone. If the alcoholic does lie, chances are that your friends and family already know that there is trouble. You need to take care of yourself and forget about everything else if you start doubting yourself. If you feel as if you are losing your mind, you need help. The person that drinks can make you feel as if it is you that is losing your mind and they are not the one telling a lie. This is very hard to take. You need help for yourself.

Handling Domestic Violence

If you live with an alcoholic, you may live with domestic violence as well. Many people that drink can become violent if they get upset. This might not be the case for some, but when a person drinks, it changes how they think. The sad thing about domestic violence where an alcoholic is concerned is that they may never display this type of behavior when they are not drinking. However, even the mildest mannered person can show signs of an entirely different person when drinking. You have to walk on eggshells when you live with someone that drinks.

The first time you are hit, may be the only time for a while, but you cannot let your guard down ever. The apologies and kindness that follows may be comforting. Nevertheless, what happens the next time the alcoholic gets angry? You could be the fault of this as well. Sometimes you do not even have to be the root of the anger and you will still be the one that is abused. Domestic violence that continues will mean that other steps must be taken.

Calling the police can aggravate a situation, but you have to get help. If you are abused, you have to report it. If this type of behavior continues, the person will be made to seek help. They might even spend some time in jail, but they will get the help that they need. It is better to call for help than let things escalate and endanger your safety more.

Judges are very helpful when sentencing time arrives. You can even talk to the prosecutor to make sure that the person receives the help that they need through a treatment program.

You need a time out away from each other. This is vital when you live with an abusive alcoholic. This means physical, mental or verbal abuse. No one should have to live with any type of abuse. If you are abused, then you need to call the police for help. The alcoholic will know that you are not going to take the abuse and the judge will know that the person needs help with his or her drinking and anger management. If you continue to let the abuse continue, you are putting your own life in danger. Just because the person is only hitting you once and a while in the back, arms or legs, does not mean that one day they will not snap and try to harm you more, or maybe even try to kill you.

Take your time and may sure that you really want him or her back home. After living with an abusive alcoholic that has gone to treatment, you still have to make sure that you can go back. If you have resentment and hatred for the person, you will not be able to live a happy life. If the person has stopped drinking, he or she may start again because of the tension in the home. You have to think long and hard before letting that person come back.

Even if an alcoholic gets help and learns to control their anger, you still may have to keep your guard up, which can lead to tension. This is not healthy for anyone including any kids in the home. You have to be sure that the abuse will not continue. You need reassurances that you might not get.

Eliminate Alcohol In The Home

When you live with an alcoholic in your life, you have to change the way you live. You have to change the way you keep your house stocked with beverages. You have to realize that having alcohol in the home is a thing of the past. An alcoholic does not care where the drink comes from as long as they can drink it. This is hard to understand for many people. If you do not have a drinking problem, but enjoy a drink occasionally, you will have to make some changes. The sad thing is that you may have to be the one to hide the alcohol.

If you drink, you have to use good judgment. You have to realize that living with an alcoholic and drinking yourself can make for some intense moments. It may make you feel superior and able to say things that you normally would not. This could create some arguments and even some abusive behavioral on both parts. If you do drink, it should be on moderation and make sure that you do not need to discuss anything with your spouse or partner when you are drinking.

Keep alcohol out of sight if you live with an alcoholic in your life. This is important, but it is also necessary. Many alcoholics will hide their empties so that you do not know that they are drinking, but now you will have to be the one hiding the alcohol if you want to keep it in the house. This now becomes a really bad living situation. Unfortunately, if you want alcohol in the house for yourself or for when guests stop over, you will have to keep it out of sight.

A lock on the liquor cabinet will not deter the alcoholic in your life. If the person knows that there is alcohol in the house, even if you use a lock and key to keep them out, they will find a way. This is sad because you want to feel safe and secure in your home, but the problem is already inside. You have to change the way you live when you live with an alcoholic. There is no easy way to keep alcoholic beverages in the house where an alcoholic lives.

If you have alcohol in the house, be prepared to have it disappear quickly. This is a problem for anyone that keeps alcohol in the house. Just because Aunt Sally brought it over for when she visits will not mean a thing. The alcoholic that needs a drink does not care whose alcohol it is but only that it is there and they need it. This can cause more problems when Aunt Sally comes for a visit and the alcohol is gone. You have to explain and tell the truth instead of covering it up.

Hiding alcohol is not the answer, but unfortunately, it is the only way you can keep alcohol in the house if you do. Sometimes you will feel like this is not worth it and get discouraged. This is the time you need to talk to someone. Living with an alcoholic that seeks and finds the alcohol to drink has a problem and most counsellors will tell you not to keep alcohol in the house at all. This is not what you want to hear, but short of sleeping with the alcohol next to your bed, this may be the only way to stop the alcoholic from drinking what is not theirs.

You may need to have an alcohol free home to deter drinking at home. This is not hard to do if you do not want a cocktail now and then. If you are just a casual drinker and only want a few cocktails, you will have to decide what is more important. This is hard, but then again, living with an alcoholic is hard most of the time. There is no easy way to live with a person that has a drinking problem. You have to make sacrifices in most cases to make things work.

Make The Effort To Attend Only Parties That Do Not Serve Alcohol

If you are living with an alcoholic that is still drinking or is attending AA or another treatment, you have to plan for the parties or events that you attend. Going to a brat fry where alcohol is served is not the best idea. Attending a wine tasting event or joining friends for a birthday party where alcohol will be served should be avoided. Your life is different when you live with an alcoholic. You try to stay away from events that serve alcohol, even a family gathering. You even change the way you have parties and hope that everyone understands.

If you are having a party, you should have a non-alcohol party. This can be hard to sell to your friends and family, but if they know the situation, they should be more than happy to attend and do without the drinking. In some cases, you might have a smaller party than you wanted. However, you have to think positive. You are doing this for the both of you and not for anyone else. It can be a touchy situation if the family and friends do not know why you are doing this.

If your guests are confused, you can explain or tell them that you do not feel it is appropriate at the time. If they understand the problem, they may be more apt to attend and have a good time without drinking. Not all of the people will accept what you are saying, but in most cases, people that care will be willing to have an alcohol free party. It can be hard for the recovering alcoholic to be around any alcohol and this is the only way you can help. If the person is still drinking, this can save from some embarrassing moments.

Try to attend parties that are not serving alcohol. This is hard if your friends and family drink. Try making some new friends that do not have to drink. In some cases, a person that attends group meetings will make friends with other members and they will enjoy doing things together with their families. This is just another way that groups help the alcoholic. If you have some other things you can do, you do them. Family picnics or even taking the kids on a hike does not require alcohol. Do things that will not tempt the person to drink.

Attend some events where alcohol is not served and have fun. You have to show him or her that you can have fun without drinking. This might be hard to do because the person may be annoyed or depressed because they would rather drink. You just have to enjoy yourself and show them that it is fun to do things without drinking. You could be fighting a losing battle, but at least you will have a few hours without someone being intoxicated. This is great if you have kids.

If you are having a child's birthday, do not serve alcohol to anyone. People always seem to have alcoholic beverages at a kids birthday parties, but you can refrain and have a party for the kids instead for the adults. Just make it known that this is a party for a kid and you do not feel that alcohol is needed. You could also explain that there are problems with alcohol in the family and you prefer to keep the party free from any drinking.

Be prepared for an attitude from the alcoholic when you attend parties with no alcohol. They can become upset, inattentive, depressed and frigidity. You can only try to enjoy yourself and try to include them in the fun. The alcoholic that needs alcohol will have to start to have fun or suffer. This is harsh, but it is the only way to show them that you are serious about enjoying things without the drinking. It is possible to get them to have fun. You just have to try and include them, but do not force them to try. They will get the picture when they see you enjoying yourself.

Change Your Own Drinking Habits

If you drink when out with friends or at home with the partner that drinks, you make have to make a change if you want the alcoholic to stop. An alcoholic cannot stop drinking if they live in a house with someone that drinks even one cocktail a week. They see you drinking and determine that if you are happy with your drinking, you should accept their drinking. If they want to stop and you drink in front of them, they will not be able to do it. An alcoholic that wants to stop cannot around someone that drinks in front of them or that goes out and comes home smelling of alcohol.

You might have to stop drinking. This is the only way that you can show your support for the alcoholic that is trying to stop drinking. It is also the only way that you can make your point that you do not want them to drink. You cannot tell someone that they cannot do something if you do it. Remember that the alcoholic does not think that they have a drinking problem. They are just drinking as you do. You have to make some changes with your own drinking habits if you want to make an appeal for the alcoholic to stop drinking.

Maybe you can go with friends somewhere else to drink when you are gone for the weekend or overnight. However, this is just another deception in your relationship. Some alcoholics do not want to stop, but if you sit and drink with them, they think that you accept their drinking. If you sneak out to drink, you are just doing what they could do. If you want to enjoy a night out, you may want to drink non-alcoholic drinks. If you do drink, you should not be preaching to the band even if you only drink occasionally.

Talk to him or her and see how they feel about your drinking. In some cases, the alcoholic knows that they have a problem and they know that you only have a few drinks here and there. They may not have a problem with this. However, if they think that because you drink, this means that they can drink, you may need to stop even if they have no problem with you drinking. This sounds ridiculous, but it can happen. Many alcoholics know they have a problem and they know that their spouse or partner does not.

Should you be supportive and hide your drinking from the alcoholic in your life? This should never be done if you want to keep the lies out of the picture. An alcoholic lies and hides their drinking when their family wants them to stop. You would be doing the exact same thing. You may want a drink sometimes, but if you do, you must not hide it. This can only cause more problems in the relationship.

If you have problems understanding why you cannot have a drink, you may have to re-examine your own feelings for the person. Sometimes a person finds it hard to change because they are not the one with the problem. This might be true, but if you live with an alcoholic, you have to make changes and sacrifices. This is just part of the problem. If you feel that you should not have to give anything up, then maybe you need to think about what you want.

If you think that giving up drinking is hard, then maybe you should. If you think that you cannot change the way you live to be with an alcoholic, then you might not be in the right relationship. Sometimes you have to make a decision that means that you cannot have a drink or you cannot go out with friends. This is a choice that you have to make. You have to be sure of what you want. Sometimes to be right, you have to stop drinking so that the alcoholic knows that you want them to do it as well.

Supporting The Alcoholic Once He Decides To Stop Drinking

If the person that you live with wants to stop drinking, you have to help as well. When an alcoholic wants to stop, you have to give up a few things that you may enjoy. The person will need your support when they are trying to stop the drinking and change. This is not easy for the person to do and you have to be the strong one again. You have to offer encouragement and not offer judgment. Judging the alcoholic that is asking for help is not going to work. You have to offer compassion and support. They are not just doing this for themselves. They are doing it for you as well.

Talk with them about what they are doing. This should be done when they are not drinking. You can calmly explain how the drinking is affecting the family. You can tell them how it has affected your children and your own feelings. In most cases, the alcoholic does not even realize what he or she has done to the family. They never take the time to see how their drinking affects anyone. All they know is that they were doing what they wanted to do.

Make sure that the person knows that you will stand by them through this time. This is probably one of the hardest things to do, but if you care about this person, you have to stand by them and offer any support that you can. If they join AA and continue to attend meetings, the 12-step program could bring up some bad memories that you do not want to hear, but you must listen and forgive or at least try. This is the hardest part of the 12-step program. It can bring back some horrible memories that could be very upsetting.

Offer to stop drinking in front of them if you drink. This is important until the alcoholic feels comfortable with what they are accomplishing. If the person is trying to refrain from drinking and attending meetings, you do not want to be drinking in front of him or her. You have to make some changes as well. You cannot sit and drink even a few cocktails in front of them because the urge to drink for them will be strong until they learn how to control those urges. They may have an urge and slip, but you could offer help there as well.

Offer to be with them whenever they feel a need to drink. If they feel the urge to drink coming, you can be there for the person. Make the thoughts and urges go away by offering to go for a walk or to take a ride. If you have never had an addiction, you cannot for a minute understand how the person feels inside. It is hard to control the urge if the person has been drinking for so long. Do something or go to a diner for a few coffees and just talk.

When the person wants to drink, think of something else the two of you could do instead.

This is the best thing you could do for someone that wants to quit drinking, but is have problems with it. You have to be strong and offer to listen or just sit and hold their hand. You have to be supportive and do whatever you can to make sure that they have another option to drinking. It is not easy to overcome an addiction, but with your support and the help of a group or treatment, they can succeed.

Looking to get your hands
on more great books?

Come visit us on the web
and check out our giant
collection of books covering
all categories and topics. We
have something for
everyone!

http://www.kmspublishing.com

KMS Publishing.com